EARTHQUAKES

Petra Miller

Cavendish

Published in 2015 by Cavendish Square Publishing, LLC
243 5th Avenue, Suite 136, New York, NY 10016

First Edition

Website: cavendishsq.com

This publication represents the opinions and views of the author based on his or her personal experience, knowledge, and research. The information in this book serves as a general guide only. The author and publisher have used their best efforts in preparing this book and disclaim liability rising directly or indirectly from the use and application of this book.

CPSIA Compliance Information: Batch #WW15CSQ

All websites were available and accurate when this book was sent to press.

Library of Congress Cataloging-in-Publication Data

Miller, Petra, author.
Earthquakes / Petra Miller.
pages cm. — (The power of nature)
Includes bibliographical references and index.
ISBN 978-1-50260-215-2 (hardcover) ISBN 978-1-50260-214-5 (ebook)
1. Earthquakes—Juvenile literature. I. Title.

QE521.3.M55 2015
551.22—dc23

2014026391

Editor: Fletcher Doyle
Copy Editor: Cynthia Roby
Art Director: Jeffrey Talbot
Designer: Joseph Macri
Senior Production Manager: Jennifer Ryder-Talbot
Production Editor: David McNamara
Photo Researcher: J8 Media

The photographs in this book are used by permission and through the courtesy of: Cover photo by Ken M Johns/Photo Researchers/Getty Images; KAZUHIRO NOGI/AFP/GettyImages, 4; POOL/AFP/ Getty Images, 6; BAY ISMOYO/AFP/Getty Images, 8; Webspark/Shutterstock.com, 11; United States Geological Survey/File:Map plate tectonics world.gif/Wikimedia Commons, 13; Andrew Green/Dorling Kindersley/Getty Images, 14; AFP/Getty Images, 17; Wichita Eagle/Getty Images, 18; AFP/Getty Images, 21; U.S. Geological Survey Photographic Library, 22; NYPL/Science Source/Photo Researchers/Getty Images, 25; Claudio Núñez/File:2010 Chile earthquake - Building destroyed in Concepción.jpg/Wikimedia Commons, 29; Otto Greule Jr/Getty Images, 30; U.S. Geological Survey Photographic Library, 32; Conny Sjostrom/Shutterstock.com, 34; U.S. Geological Survey Photographic Library, 36; Skip ODonnel/E+/Getty Images, 39.

Printed in the United States of America

CONTENTS

Many people were left homeless by the 2011 earthquake in Japan.

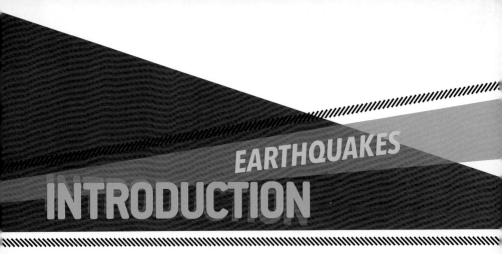

On March 11, 2011, an earthquake that registered 9.0 on the **Richter scale** rocked the northeast coast of Japan. It was one of only five earthquakes to exceed 9.0 in the last 100-plus years. Japan's early-warning system was able to detect the seismic activity about one minute before Tokyo started to feel the impact of the event. One minute does not seem like much time, but it was enough to save many lives. The residents of the city received text messages announcing the earthquake, and Japan's early-warning system halted all trains and factory production lines. However, the system could not halt the secondary natural disaster that resulted from the earthquake.

Within an hour of the earthquake, the first of numerous **tsunami** waves struck the country's eastern coast. More than 200 square miles (518 square kilometers) of Japan were flooded, drowning residents, destroying buildings, and most problematic of all, causing the meltdown of the Fukushima Daiichi Nuclear Power Plant. More than three years after the meltdown, the plant continued to contaminate water in the Pacific Ocean.

Reactor number 3 was destroyed at the Fukushima Daiichi Nuclear Power Plant.

More than eighteen thousand people died as a result of the earthquake and the tsunami waves that followed. Hundreds of thousands of Japanese citizens lost their homes.

Many were living in temporary housing years after the crisis, according to the government. The effects of the earthquake were not just limited to Japan. Europe, North America, South America, and Antarctica either felt the **seismic waves** of the earthquake or waves from the tsunami. Tsunami waves often start when an earthquake causes the ocean floor to rise or fall quickly. According to geologists, the earthquake actually affected the planet's rotation, and shortened the day by a microsecond.

Every year Earth experiences several million earthquakes. Luckily, the overwhelming majority of them are not as powerful as the event that rocked Japan. Most are so mild, or occur in unpopulated regions, that they go unnoticed. There are about sixteen earthquakes that measure 7.0 or higher on the Richter scale each year. According to the United States Geological Survey, the United States experienced only eight earthquakes 7.0 or higher from 2000 to 2012.

Many buildings were destroyed in the city of Banda Aceh when the earthquake and tsunami devastated Sumatra.

CHAPTER ONE
EARTH-MOVING EXPERIENCES

The catastrophic earthquake in Japan was not the worst earthquake of the twenty-first century. That unfortunate title goes to a 9.1 earthquake that hit the west coast of the Indonesian island of Sumatra in 2004. Like the Japanese earthquake of 2011, it also triggered a massive tsunami that swamped the island. The death toll was far worse than the Japanese disaster, with the Sumatra earthquake leading to more than 230,000 deaths. Throughout the capital city of Banda Aceh, buildings were permanently damaged. Other cities were entirely washed away.

For centuries, human beings have tried to figure out why earthquakes happen. We take for granted that we have solid ground underneath us. When that solid ground suddenly begins shaking and breaking apart, we want to know why. We also want to know if and when it will happen again.

Tectonic Plates

Earth is made up of three layers of rock, the **core**, **mantle**, and **crust**. The center of Earth is called the core. The core is made of solid rock surrounded by a layer of hot, liquid rock. The middle section is called the mantle. The mantle is made mostly of solid rock with small areas of liquid rock. The topmost layer is called the crust. Made of solid rock, the crust covers Earth's surface like a shell.

Earth's crust is broken into nine larger, and at least twelve smaller, slabs of rock. These slabs, which can be up to 62 miles (100 kilometers) thick, are called **tectonic plates**. Tectonic plates are constantly moving, either pulling away from or pushing against one another. The plates move very slowly, so you cannot actually feel the ground moving. However, as tectonic plates move, they scrape against each other. Some plates run into each other head-on. Some plates slide past each other and then become stuck. Plates also can rub against each other for long periods of time. Earthquakes begin in the Earth's crust where these plates meet.

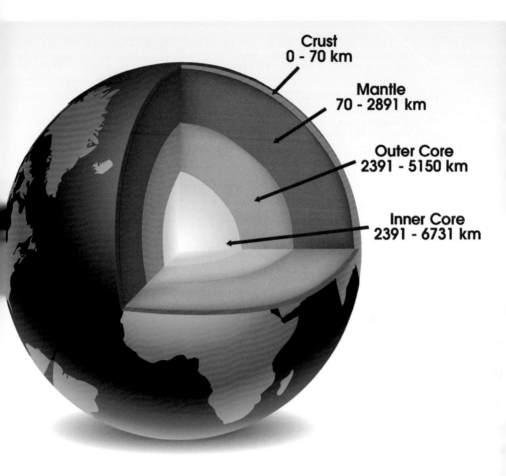

Crust
0 - 70 km

Mantle
70 - 2891 km

Outer Core
2391 - 5150 km

Inner Core
2391 - 6731 km

The crust is the thinnest of the Earth's layers.

Fractures in the Earth

The place where tectonic plates meet is called a
fault. Faults are fractures, or cracks, in Earth's
crust. Faults are a result of tectonic plates
colliding over millions of years. The plates are
put under so much strain that, eventually, they
crack. Large blocks of rock then shift past each

other along the crack. The rock on one side of the crack will shift up, down, or sideways as the rock on the other side shifts in the opposite direction. This rock movement creates an area with a lot of faults. An area with many faults is called a **fault zone**.

DID YOU KNOW?

While the San Andreas Fault is probably the U.S. fault line everyone associates with earthquake activity, there is also a major fault line which runs from St. Louis, Missouri, to Memphis, Tennessee, known as the New Madrid fault zone.

The length of a fault can range from inches to thousands of miles. The greater the fault's size, the greater the chance of an earthquake occurring. A large fault may also signal that the size of the earthquake will be large, too.

Creating Earthquakes

Over time, as tectonic plates grind against each other, pressure begins to build. As the plates push against each other, they begin to crack.

The stress on the plates becomes so great that Earth needs a way to release the pressure. This release comes in the form of a sudden burst of energy. Usually the stored-up energy will be released at the weakest point of Earth's crust. The weakest point is on a fault, where there is already a crack in the crust. The burst of energy causes a section of the fault to break loose. Then the two halves of the fault bounce past each other. This rock movement creates the strong shaking of an earthquake.

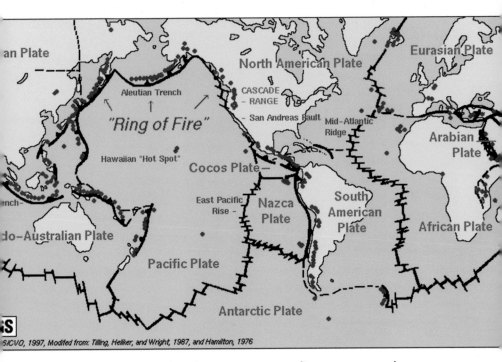

Earthquakes and volcanoes (in red) are created when tectonic plates slide past each other or collide. This happens most often along the Ring of Fire.

SHOCK WAVES

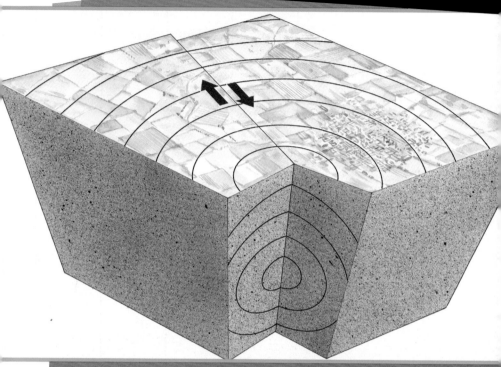

Shock waves move up and out from an earthquake's epicenter.

The burst of energy that is released by the fault comes in waves of motion. These waves are called seismic waves, or shock waves. Shock waves occur when the pressure between tectonic plates is released. Shock waves cause the earth to **vibrate** (shake) violently, which is what we feel on Earth's surface as an earthquake.

Shock waves are invisible. If you could see them, they would look like waves in an ocean. You may not be able to see shock waves, but you certainly can feel them. The shock waves of large earthquakes are very powerful. They start from the center of the earthquake, which is called the **epicenter**. Shock waves travel upward and outward from the epicenter in a circular motion. They travel through the ground extremely fast. Shock waves can cover a distance of 100 miles (161 km) in a matter of a few seconds. Sometimes these waves can be felt hundreds of miles from the earthquake's epicenter.

The shock waves can also pound soil saturated with water in a process called **liquefaction**. The shaking weakens the soil so it can no longer hold up buildings and bridges. In the 1989 California earthquake, the worst damage came in the San Francisco Marina district, where mud and sand had not been compacted properly. After liquefaction, the soil there could not support the buildings. The buildings then toppled into the slush, which acted like quicksand.

Different Types of Shocks

Earthquakes occur in sequences. An earthquake may begin with **foreshocks**. Foreshocks are small **tremors**, or vibrations, that are created when faults begin to release pressure. Foreshocks indicate that a larger **mainshock** will hit. The mainshock is the actual main earthquake.

After a major or even a moderate mainshock, smaller earthquakes usually occur. These smaller quakes are called **aftershocks**. Aftershocks happen when an earthquake does not relieve all of the pressure that has built up in the rocks of Earth's crust.

After the mainshock, aftershocks can continue over a period of weeks, months, or years. While the aftershocks will not be as powerful as the original earthquake, they are still capable of causing damage, particularly when an area has already suffered from the mainshock.

A destructive earthquake in Chile on
April 3, 2014, had a 7.6-magnitude aftershock.

The practice of hydraulic fracturing may be behind the large increase in earthquakes in Oklahoma and nearby states in 2014.

CHAPTER TWO

MEASURING EARTHQUAKES

Throughout early 2014, the state of Oklahoma was hit with a large number of earthquakes. This surprised residents, who were more used to tornadoes. In the years before 2008, Oklahoma averaged an earthquake a year. However, through the first half of 2014, occurrences of earthquakes increased to about one a day. While most of the incidents measured less than 4.5 on the Richter scale and did not cause significant property damage, the sharp increase in numbers left residents looking for answers.

Some residents and scientists have started to wonder whether the controversial practice known as hydraulic fracturing, or "fracking" for short, has created this instability in the Earth. Fracking is the process of drilling and injecting fluid into the ground at a high pressure. This process fractures, or breaks, shale rocks to release the natural gas inside.

Residents of neighboring states, particularly Texas and Kansas, are also asking the same question. Both states have also experienced a rise in the number of earthquakes.

Some earthquakes are much more powerful than the minor tremors that these three states experienced. They break up the earth with the strength of thousands of bombs and can be felt hundreds of miles from the center of the quake. These quakes cause millions of dollars of property damage and kill many people.

Many earthquakes harm no one. The tremors are too small to be felt. Even large earthquakes can be harmless if they strike in an area where no one lives.

The Work of Seismologists

Scientists who study earthquakes and vibrations in Earth are called **seismologists**. One instrument they use is called a **seismograph**. A seismograph determines the time and the place that an earthquake occurs. It also measures the quake's strength. A seismograph gives us this data by recording the motion of the ground during an earthquake.

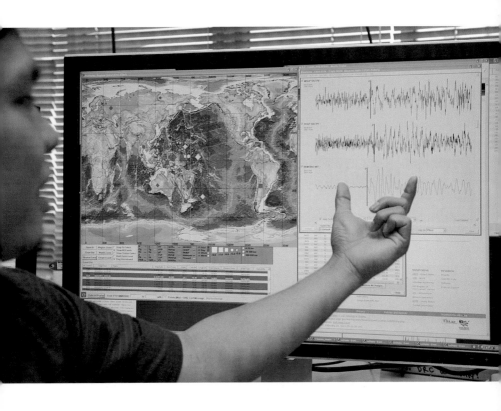

A seismograph has a frame with a needle and a long sheet of paper attached. As the ground shakes, the needle draws lines on the paper to show the vibrations. These vibrations are the seismic waves that occur during an earthquake. The seismograph records these vibrations over a specific period of time. When the movement is very strong, the needle makes a long line. The more powerful the quake, the longer the lines and the closer they are together.

Seismologists then compare this data with the data from past earthquakes. This

Government Hill Elementary School in Anchorage was destroyed in the 1964 Alaska earthquake.

The U.S. Geological Survey (USGS) catalogued this list of the ten largest earthquakes since 1900.

1. **Chile (magnitude 9.5); May 22, 1960** More than 1,600 people died and 2,000 were injured.

2. **Alaska, United States (magnitude 9.2); March 27, 1964** The Great Alaska Earthquake resulted in 131 deaths.

3. **Sumatra, Indonesia (magnitude 9.1); December 26, 2004** This catastrophe displaced about 1.7 million people.

4. **Honshu, Japan (magnitude 9.0); March 11, 2011** The ongoing legacy of this event is the nuclear crisis.

5. **Kamchatka (magnitude 9.0); November 4, 1952** Thousands of Russians died in the tsunami.

6. **Chile (magnitude 8.8); February 27, 2010** More than five hundred people died.

7. **Ecuador (magnitude 8.8); January 31, 1906** Tsunami waves hit Ecuador, Japan, San Francisco, and Colombia.

8. **Alaska (magnitude 8.8); February 3, 1965** There was no significant property damage due to low population density.

9. **Northern Sumatra, Indonesia (magnitude 8.6); March 28, 2005** This earthquake/tsunami combination killed more than one thousand.

10. **Tibet (magnitude 8.6); August 15, 1950** The death toll was placed at more than 750 people.

comparison allows seismologists to track the number of earthquakes that occur around a particular fault. This data can help seismologists to predict when another, larger quake might occur.

Determining the Size of an Earthquake

Another job of seismologists is to determine the **magnitude** of an earthquake. Magnitude is the measure of an earthquake's size. Seismologists use a system called the Richter scale to measure magnitude. Scientists Charles F. Richter and Beno Gutenberg invented the Richter scale in 1935.

The Richter scale places an earthquake's magnitude on a scale of 1 to 10. Most earthquakes measure less than a 2.5 on the Richter scale. These earthquakes are too small to cause any serious damage. A hundred of these earthquakes might occur around the world in a single hour. Usually, a quake must be in the moderate range before it can be felt.

On the Richter scale, a one-point change indicates that a quake is ten times as strong. So, with every one-point change, the

Our scale for measuring earthquakes was named for American seismologist Charles Francis Richter.

magnitude is multiplied by ten. In other words, a quake with a magnitude of 7 has one hundred times the shaking motion of a magnitude 5 quake.

The Richter scale is useful for measuring the force of an earthquake. It does not, however, always reflect the damage done. For example, if a major earthquake (7–7.9) hit a desert that had no people or buildings, it would not cause a lot of damage. However, a moderate earthquake

(5–5.9) might cause more severe damage if it hit a large city. To measure the amount of damage done by an earthquake, scientists use the **Mercalli scale.**

Measuring Earthquake Damage with the Mercalli Scale

The Mercalli scale was invented in 1931 by American seismologists Frank Neumann and Harry Wood. It was created to measure the effects of an earthquake on people and structures. The earthquakes are measured on a scale of 1 to 12 using Roman numerals (I–XII). The higher the number on the Mercalli scale, the more destructive the earthquake has been.

For example, on the Mercalli scale, a number III (three) means that hanging objects may swing. The vibration felt would be the same as that from a large truck driving nearby. Most people won't recognize it as a quake. However, a number IX (nine) means buildings will be damaged, many will likely collapse. Underground pipes will have broken.

The Mercalli scale also measures how an earthquake is felt in different areas. For example, during California's Loma Prieta

Richter	Mercalli	Earthquake Effects
	I	**Instrumental**. Not felt except by a very few under especially favourable conditions detected mostly by seismography.
2	II	**Feeble**. Felt only by a few persons at rest, especially on upper floors of buildings.
	III	**Slight**. Felt quite noticeable by persons indoors especially on upper floors of buildings. Many people do not recognize it as an earthquake. Standing motor cars may rock slightly. Vibration similar to the passing of a truck.
3	IV	**Moderate**. Felt indoors by many, outdoors by few during the day. At night, some awakening. Dishes, windows, doors disturbed; walls made cracking sound. Sensation like a heavy truck striking building. Standing motor cars rocked noticeably.
4	V	**Rather Strong**. Felt by nearly everyone; many awakened. Some dishes, windows broken. Unstable objects overturned. Pendulum clocks may stop.
	VI	**Strong**. Felt by all, many frightened. Some heavy furniture moved; a few instances of fallen plaster. Damage slight.
5	VII	**Very Strong**. Damage negligible in buildings of good design and construction; slight to moderate in well-built ordinary structures; considerable damage in ordinary structures; considerable damage in poorly built or badly designed structures.
6	VIII	**Destructive**. Damage slight in specially designed structures; considerable damage in ordinary substantial buildings with partial collapse. Damage great in poorly built structures. Fall of factory stacks, columns, monuments, walls. Heavy furniture overturned.
7	IX	**Ruinous**. Damage considerable in specially design structures; well-designed frame structures thrown out of plumb. Damage great in substantial buildings, with partial collapse. Buildings shifted off foundations.
	X	**Disastrous**. Some well-built wooden structures destroyed; most masonry and frame structures destroyed with foundations. Rails bent greatly.
8+	XI	**Very Disastrous**. Few, if any (masonry) structures remain standing. Bridges destroyed. Rails bent greatly.
	XII	**Catastrophic**. Damage total. Lines of sight and level are destroyed. Objects thrown into the air.

ormation courtesy of dmca.gov.ms

The Richter scale measures an earthquake's magnitude; the Mercalli scale measures its effects.

Earthquake (1989), some of the worst damage happened more than 70 miles (113 k) from the epicenter in the Santa Cruz Mountains. This can be attributed to the soil conditions in the hardest-hit areas. Some areas close to the epicenter had much lower Mercalli numbers than those in the San Francisco Bay area.

Different area ratings on the Mercalli Scale help in plotting damage patterns. A map showing the Mercalli intensity at different locations for the same earthquake can be revealing. When damage is compared to geological maps, underlying rocks and their affect on the earthquake's intensity can be seen.

The 2010 earthquake in Chile caused severe
damage in the capital city of Santiago.

The 1989 World Series was delayed ten days because of an earthquake, although baseball fans at Candlestick Park in San Francisco were safe.

Fans tuning in to watch Game Three of the 1989 World Series between the San Francisco Giants and the Oakland A's instead witnessed the devastation of Loma Prieta, an earthquake measuring 6.9 on the Richter scale. The broadcast was interrupted just minutes after the game's opening. The announcer, Al Michaels, began to inform the audience of what was happening but was cut off halfway through the word "earthquake." Within a few minutes, sound was restored, and Michaels was able to keep the worldwide television audience up-to-date.

Baseball fans at the stadium remained safe. Unfortunately, more than sixty people were killed and thousands were injured in the region. An elevated highway collapsed in Oakland, crushing cars and killing passengers. Loma Prieta was the area's most damaging earthquake since the 1906 San Francisco earthquake that killed thousands and obliterated entire towns north of San Francisco. The World Series was delayed ten days as the area recovered.

A section of Interstate 880 in Oakland collapsed in the 1989 earthquake.

By 1989, scientists had better technology to learn about earthquakes than they did in 1906. Since the Loma Prieta earthquake, technology has improved even more. Seismologists still cannot predict exactly when and where a quake will occur, but new technology is improving their calculations. Seismologists now have high-tech meters that are buried in faults. The meters measure the activity near a particular fault and the amount of pressure that is building around it. This could allow scientists to provide earthquake warnings more than ten hours before one happens. Seismologists are also experimenting with lasers and **global positioning satellite systems** to develop models of faults. These tools help scientists to study plate movement. The more seismologists know about plate movement, the better they can predict when and where a quake may happen. Today's scientists use **plate tectonics** (the study of plate movement) to predict where 90 percent of Earth's major earthquakes are likely to occur.

Scientists also study the number of earthquakes that have happened in an area to predict if and when another quake will occur. For example, there were four major earthquakes in the San Francisco Bay Area between 1979 and 1989. Seismologists believe this quake activity means that the San Andreas Fault is becoming less stable. Scientists predict that there is a 63 percent chance that a major earthquake (magnitude 7 or larger) will strike the area by 2036. With about three hundred large fault lines running beneath it, California is one of the most seismically active parts of the world, and has 37,000 tremors a year.

People walk through the rift valley, formed in Iceland's Thingvellir National Park by tectonic plates pulling away from each other.

Predicting Earthquakes

Today's scientists are sure enough about their predictions to issue earthquake warnings. These warnings alert local governments and residents to prepare for a large earthquake. Warnings also give search-and-rescue teams time to organize.

Earthquake warnings are not as accurate as those issued for other natural disasters, such as hurricanes. Earthquake forecasting is a new science based on the probability of an earthquake striking within a period of time.

For example, in June 1988, a magnitude 5.1 quake hit just outside San Francisco. Scientists determined that there was a one-in-twenty chance that a bigger quake would occur in the next five days. Earthquake warnings were issued, but nothing happened. One year later, another small quake struck the same area. Once again, the warning period went by with no earthquake activity. However, sixty-nine days later, the area was struck by the Loma Prieta earthquake. Sixty-three people died. The region suffered $6 billion in damages.

Scientists were about two months off in their warnings, but local governments still found them helpful. They practiced what the different city departments would do in the event of a quake. When the quake did finally strike, emergency teams were prepared.

Making Buildings Earthquake Proof

Scientists try to predict not only when an earthquake will occur, but also how much damage it will cause. They study the types of structures near faults. Many deaths caused by

Sea life, once underwater, changes color on shoreline rocks raised by the 1964 Alaska earthquake.

The earthquake that hit Alaska in 1964 was the largest ever in the United States. It taught us most of what we know today about what causes these disasters. Before then, the idea that Earth's plates are moving and colliding, creating mountains, volcanoes, and earthquakes, was a theory that many people doubted.

Geologist George Plafker of the United States Geological Survey was sent to Alaska after the earthquake. There he observed islands in Prince William Sound that had been lifted 38 feet (11.6 meters). He explored areas where the sea floor had been raised, exposing barnacle-covered rocks that were turning white. He also saw areas where forests had dropped below the high tide line. The trees were being killed by the saltwater.

The deformation of the land was so great that Plafker was able to make scientific observations not available before. On the Pacific Rim, where most megathrust (one plate going beneath another) earthquakes occur, the plates usually meet under the ocean so the rising and falling of Earth's surface is out of view. The only explanation for the data was that one tectonic plate, the Pacific, went underneath another plate, the North American, causing some areas to rise and others to fall.

This discovery led to the creation of the National Earthquake Information Center and helped explain how tsunamis are started.

earthquakes are because of badly constructed buildings. Scientists now help **architects** design buildings that will hold up during a quake.

Architects use materials that can bend or sway, such as steel, to construct buildings and bridges. Structures made from materials that are not **flexible**, such as bricks, can fall apart quickly from a shock wave.

Earthquake Survival Tips

The most important step of earthquake survival is preparation. Discussing a plan with your family and building a disaster kit is a great first step. Your kit should contain water, food, and medical supplies to last at least 72 hours.

DID YOU KNOW?

Thanks to the motion of the San Andreas Fault, San Francisco is moving toward Los Angeles at the rate of 2 inches (5.08 centimeters) a year. The two cities will meet in several million years.

If an earthquake strikes and you are inside, stay away from glass, windows, or doors to the outside. Get under a table, and hold on until the shaking stops. Stay inside until an adult tells you it is safe to move.

If you are outdoors, move to an open area away from any structures. Drivers should stop their cars when clear of any objects that can fall, such as a bridge over the road.

If you are trapped under debris, don't try to move it. You may make things worse. Cover your mouth to avoid inhaling dust and wait for rescue.

Families in earthquake-prone areas should pack an emergency kit.

GLOSSARY

aftershock A smaller earthquake that happens after the main earthquake.

architect A person who designs homes and other buildings.

core The center of Earth, made of solid rock and surrounded by a layer of hot, liquid rock.

crust The topmost layer of Earth.

epicenter The center of an earthquake and the point from which shock waves start.

fault A fracture or crack in Earth's crust.

fault zone An area with many closely spaced faults.

flexible Able to bend and return to its original position.

foreshock A small tremor or vibration that is created when plates begin to crack.

global positioning satellite systems Instruments that help seismologists study plate movement in Earth's crust.

liquefaction The process of making or becoming liquid; conversion of a solid into a liquid by heat, or of a gas into a liquid by cold or pressure.

magnitude The size and intensity of an earthquake as measured by the Richter scale.

mainshock The strongest in a series of earthquakes.

mantle The middle layer of Earth, made mostly of solid rock with small areas of liquid rock.

Mercalli scale The way to measure a quake's damage potential, based on a Roman numeral system.

plate tectonics The study of tectonic plate movement.

Richter scale The way of measuring the magnitude of an earthquake; named for Charles F. Richter.

seismic waves Invisible shock waves that travel outward from the epicenter of an earthquake.

seismograph An instrument used to record the vibrations of an earthquake.

seismologist A scientist who studies earthquakes and their phenomena.

tectonic plates Slabs of rock that make up Earth's crust.

tremor Shaking in the ground caused by an earthquake.

tsunami An extremely large wave that can be caused by an earthquake in the ocean floor.

vibrate To move or cause to move continuously and rapidly to and fro.

FURTHER INFORMATION

Books

Furgang, Kathy. *Everything Volcanoes and Earthquakes*. National Geographic Kids. New York, NY: National Geographic Children's Books, 2013.

Griffey, Harriet. *Earthquakes and Other Natural Disasters*. DK Readers. New York, NY: DK Publishing, 2011.

Higgins, Nadia. *Natural Disasters Through Infographics*. Super Science Infographics. Minneapolis, MN: Lerner Publishing Group, 2013.

Kerrod, Robin. *Exploring Science: Volcanoes & Earthquakes*. Exploring Science. Chapel Hill, NC: Armadillo Books, 2014.

Live Science: 13 Crazy Earthquake Facts

www.livescience.com/6187-13-crazy-earthquake-facts.html

Did you know that San Francisco is moving toward Los Angeles at the rate of about 2 inches (5.08 cm) per year? This is the same pace as the growth of your fingernails. Did you know that an earthquake on one side of Earth can shake the other side? Visit this website to learn more interesting information and trivia about earthquakes and view lots of fun photos.

Ready.gov: Earthquake Preparedness Site

www.ready.gov/earthquakes

Explore the basics of earthquakes and discover resources covering how to prepare for such an event, as well as how to become involved in your community to increase overall preparedness. Play games that will test your know-how in a wide range of emergencies and teach you how to build the perfect emergency kit.

USGS: Earthquake Hazard Program
earthquake.usgs.gov/
earthquakes/?source=sitenav
Discover earthquake facts, maps of the most
recent earthquakes, real-time information
about earthquake activity both in the
United States and around the world, and
more!

INDEX